American Legends: The Life of John Wayne

By Charles River Editors

John Wayne & Marsha Hunt in Born to the West (1937)

About Charles River Editors

Introduction

John Wayne (1907-1979)

"Every country in the world loved the folklore of the West -- the music, the dress, the excitement, everything that was associated with the opening of a new territory. It took everybody out of their own little world. The cowboy lasted a hundred years, created more songs and prose and poetry than any other folk figure. The closest thing was the Japanese samurai. Now, I wonder who'll continue it." – John Wayne

A lot of ink has been spilled covering the lives of history's most influential figures, but how much of the forest is lost for the trees? In Charles River Editors' American Legends series, readers can get caught up to speed on the lives of America's most important men and women in the time it takes to finish a commute, while learning interesting facts long forgotten or never known.

Hollywood has produced no shortage of famous movie stars, but none have been as culturally significant as John Wayne. Marion Morrison was born in a quintessentially quaint Midwestern town, but he eventually grew up to become John Wayne, the legend of the silver screen who embodied the Western frontier. Wayne starred in so many movies (nearly 150 in all) that when asked to name his worst, he joked that 50 of them were tied, but the excessive number allowed Wayne to portray heroes of all stripes, from cowboys to soldiers, and he was invariably charming, courageous, and full of rugged, masculine swagger.

Even as Westerns have certainly waned in popularity, Wayne himself has remained immensely popular, in part because he set the prototype for the heroic character, regardless of genre. Wayne will always be associated with Westerns, John Wayne transcended the Western genre. Through the portrayal of rugged, masculine characters, Wayne came to epitomize the American spirit and the way Americans view themselves. In that sense, he is truly America's actor, and he continues to live on in both the reels of Hollywood's archives and the living rooms of middle America.

At the same time, the central role of John Wayne in defining a big piece of American culture is not without controversy. His later interview with Playboy magazine is a case in point. Many Americans today realize that John Wayne's America, though beloved by many, is not the America that everyone calls their own. Western movies that pay homage to Confederate soldiers and Indian-killing frontiersman and cowboys are not everyone's cup of tea.

American Legends: The Life of John Wayne looks at the iconic actor's life on and off the silver screen, from his outsized influence to Hollywood to his outspoken views on politics. Along with pictures of important people, places, and events, you will learn about The Duke like you never have before, in no time at all.

John Wayne in *The Challenge of Ideas* (1961)

Chapter 1: Marion Morrison

"If everything isn't black and white, I say, 'Why the hell not?'" - John Wayne

On May 26, 1907, the man who would become The Duke was born Marion Robert Morrison Winterset, Iowa, a quaint country town that epitomized the rural Midwest. Though this wasn't the slice of "Americana" that would come to define his legacy, it had an enduring impact on Morrison's life.

Marion was the eldest of two children born to Clyde and Mary Morrison, who were of Scots-Irish and Scottish decent. Clyde's father (and his son's namesake), Marion Mitchell Morrison, was a veteran of the Civil War, and young Marion Robert had his middle name changed to Mitchell when his parents decided they wanted to name their next son Robert.

Clyde and Mary raised their children in the Presbyterian Church, and Clyde attempted to become a farmer in Iowa. Living amid seas of corn, it seemed a logical way to make a living. Unfortunately, Clyde's Midwestern roots were unhelpful in guiding his farm pursuits, and when his farm quickly failed, it left the Morrison family down and out. Worse, Clyde developed a lung condition which he thought was made worse by the cold and often brutal climate in rural Iowa. A new location seemed necessary.

Without a means to make any money, the family considered the classic American method of self-improvement: heading west. The Morrisons kept moving, crossing the North American continent until they reached its farthest western reach - California. This classic venture – a family trekking across North America – inevitably played an enormous role in young Marion's life. His later career in the movies must have been filled with nostalgia, replaying the most beloved and earliest days of his childhood life.

Moreover, the idea of having to pull oneself up by the bootstraps and rely on individual determination might certainly have been planted during these early years. Decades later, after he had become one of the most famous people in the world, he gave candid opinions on the idea of welfare in an interview with Playboy that might have reflected how he viewed his father's plight before the social safety net started by Franklin Roosevelt's New Deal:

"I know all about that. In the late Twenties, when I was a sophomore at USC, I was a socialist myself — but not when I left. The average college kid idealistically wishes everybody could have ice cream and cake for every meal. But as he gets older and gives more thought to his and his fellow man's responsibilities, he finds that it can't work out that way — that some people just won't carry their load ... I believe in welfare — a welfare work program. I don't think a fella should be able to sit on his backside and receive welfare. I'd like to know why well-educated idiots keep apologizing for lazy and complaining people who think the world owes them a living. I'd like to know why they make excuses for cowards who spit in the faces of the police and then run behind the judicial sob sisters. I can't understand these people who carry placards to save the life of some criminal, yet have no thought for the innocent victim."

Once they arrived in the warmer climate of Southern California, Clyde considered giving farming a second try. This time, however, ranching was Clyde's chosen method of farming. But living amidst the Mojave Desert, an obviously less farm-friendly climate than Iowa, did not improve Clyde's chances of success. His ranch failed once again, making the family's trip to California seem completely fruitless.

The family then relocated to a more metropolitan part of California, where Clyde completely changed careers and became a pharmacist. With that, 10 year old Marion and his family finally had a home, but the youngster now also had a clear purpose for his family, delivering medicines for his father. The job was his first, and it allowed him to earn some extra money and no doubt instilled the value of hard work. Clyde also clearly instilled a tough mentality in his son, who later recounted, "I've always followed my father's advice: He told me, first, to always keep my word and, second, to never insult anybody unintentionally. If I insult you, you can be goddamn sure I intend to. And, third, he told me not to go around looking for trouble."

During this time, young Marion earned his first nickname: "Little Duke." Along one of Marion's delivery routes, a resident had a huge dog named Duke. Marion was scared of the dog and preferred to stay off the grounds of the residence. Noticing this, the resident, a fireman, decided to give Morrison the name Duke. Preferring "Duke" to Marion, the name stuck.

Others suggest another origin for the Duke nickname is Marion's own dog. In this account, Marion spent so much time, not so little time, with his own pet dog, a huge Airedale Terrior named Duke, that the pair became Little and Big Duke. Whatever the origins of the name, one fact is clear: Marion Morrison was not interested in his given name and would change it repeatedly throughout his life. Duke would be but the first of many nicknames.

At school, Little Duke excelled both in the classroom and outside of it. Along with his high grades, he participated in numerous extracurricular activities, including school government and varsity football, two sides that both contributed to young Duke's all-American character. In 1924, Duke was on the champion football team of his high school, Glendale High. Despite finding time to lead his school to a regional football victory and participate in student government, it was the theater that occupied the bulk of Duke's interests. He participated in many school plays and was a star actor from an early age.

As his high school years came to a close, he had to consider where to go next. First on his list was the U.S. Naval Academy, but his hopes were dashed when he was rejected from the prestigious academy. Instead, he found a home elsewhere, the University of Southern California (USC), receiving an athletic scholarship to go play football.

Chapter 2: Becoming an Actor

"I've worked in a business where it's almost a requirement to break your word if you want to survive."

At the University of Southern California, Duke largely continued his high school pursuits. Duke's interests truly were eclectic. Though he was an avid athlete and on the football team, he also enjoyed theater, drama, politics and the law. His chosen major was pre-law, in anticipation of later attending law school. Duke was also popular on campus, and was a member of various Greek fraternities, including the Trojan Knights and Sigma Chi.

Duke's matriculation at USC, however, was cut short. During a bodysurfing expedition on the shores of Southern California, Duke suffered an injury that forced him to leave the football team. Unfortunately, his entire education relied on his playing for the team, since his athletic scholarship was naturally based on his participation for the football team. Duke was so terrified of admitting what happened to his coach that he refused to tell him, but because he had to leave the team, he also lost his scholarship, and without the funds he was unable to continue studying at the University of Southern California.

Despite what appeared to be a setback, this freed up time for the young man to focus on other things, namely his love of theater, drama and a new form of media: film. To make some cash, hopefully with the intent of returning to USC, Duke found his first introduction to film. Even at USC, he had combined his football interest with his fascination with drama to land a job working as a football character extra in a couple of films, including *Brown of Harvard* (1926) and *Drop Kick* (1927). He recruited some of his fellow football players to join him in these screenings, but now that he was no longer at USC, Duke was on his own.

Duke's football connections helped him in another crucial way. Long before he actually started starring before the camera, much of Duke's early "career" in film didn't include a place on the screen. Often, he would be charged with more mundane tasks, like moving furniture or props and helping organize the filming of a piece. In fact, it had all started as a summer job that Western silent film star Tom Mix got Duke as a quid-pro-quo in exchange for tickets to USC football games.

Tom Mix

During the late 1920's and early 1930's, Duke took up work as an extra full-time. In 1928, he was an extra in *Mother Machree*, where he met a critical and rising star among film directors: John Ford. The pair became friends, a connection which would soon propel Duke's career in film to unprecedented heights. Still, most of Duke's film work during this period was done with the Fox Film Corporation, and he was credited as Duke Morrison on films like *Word and Music* (1929). This name would not last much longer, nor would his status as an extra.

John Ford

Right as the United States was grappling with its worst economic tumult in its history, the Great Depression, Duke was experiencing more progress in acting than ever before. Oddly enough, Duke got his big break while performing menial tasks on set. While moving props around on stage, a famous director named Raoul Walsh noticed Duke and invited him to audition for a starring role in an upcoming film, the *Big Trail* (1930). The film, a Western about settlers heading west during the mid-19th century, was right up Duke's alley, given his own life story. With the Great Depression displacing Americans from coast to coast, Walsh thought it would be a hit, and that Duke was perfect for the spot.

Raoul Walsh (center)

Instead of casting Duke as "Duke Morrison," Walsh thought a name like "Anthony Wayne" would be more fitting. Though Walsh came up with that name based off "Mad Anthony" Wayne, a Revolutionary War hero, Winfield Sheehan at Fox Studios thought it sounded too Italian, which wouldn't play as well with American audiences. In response, Walsh came up with John Wayne, a compromise that all parties eventually agreed would be the perfect name. Ironically, none of those parties included Duke, who had no say and was not part of the deliberations. Nevertheless, the actor and the rest of the world was about to be introduced to a new name, even if the man bearing the name never quite got used to it:

"Republic Pictures gave me a screen credit on one of the early pictures and called me Michael Burn. On another one, they called me Duke Morrison. Then they decided Duke Morrison didn't have enough prestige. My real name, Marion Michael Morrison, didn't sound American enough for them. So they came up with John Wayne, I didn't have any say in it, but I think it's a great name. It's short and strong and to the point. It took me a long time to get used to it, though. I still don't recognize it when somebody calls me John."

Chapter 3: John Wayne

"His milieu is still the action Western, in which Wayne's simplistic plotlines and easily discernible good and bad guys attest to a romantic way of life long gone from the American scene—if indeed it ever really existed. Even his screen name—changed from Marion Michael Morrison—conveys the man's plain, rugged cinematic personality." - Playboy

The Big Trail was aptly named, because it was a historically big production for the time. The production of the movie cost over $2 million dollars, a fortune in any era but especially during the height of the Great Depression. It also broke barriers in the history of film by becoming one of the first films to be shot outdoors with sound. On top of all that, it also used a new time of film: 70 mm Grandeur.

According to Wayne, he almost lost his starring role in the film. When Wayne was asked in the Playboy magazine if it was unfamiliar for him "looking like an idiot", he recalled a humorous anecdote on the set of *The Big Trail*, which was shot on location in the Southwest:

"One of the times I really felt like a fool was when I was working on my first important film, The Big Trail, in Yuma, Arizona. I was three weeks flat on my back with turistas—or Montezuma's revenge, or the Aztec two-step, whatever you want to call it. You know, you get a little grease and soap on the inside of a fork and you've got it. Anyway, that was the worst case I ever had in my life. I'd been sick for so long that they finally said. "Jeez, Duke, if you can't get up now, we've got to get somebody else to take your place." So, with a loss of 18 pounds, I returned to work. My first scene was carrying in an actor named Tully Marshall, who was known to booze it up quite a bit. He had a big jug in his hand in this scene, and I set him down and we have a drink with another guy. They passed the jug to me first, and I dug back into it; it was straight rotgut bootleg whiskey. I'd been puking and crapping blood for a week and now I just poured that raw stuff right down my throat. After the scene, you can bet I called him every kind of an old bastard."

While the movie broke barriers in film production and was later added by Congress to the National Film Register as "culturally, historically, or aesthetically significant", *The Big Trail* fell short of breaking any records at the box office. In fact, the film was a flop and sold few tickets. This was partly due to the Grandeur film, which many theaters were unequipped to support, and frankly the Great Depression cut back on luxuries and non-essential spending for a large percentage of the population.

Regardless, it was a huge disappointment for the newly-minted John Wayne, and it put his acting career temporarily on hold. After the failure of *The Big Trail*, Wayne was given lesser roles in films, and would not star for some time. Among his more interesting roles during this period was a corpse in *The Deceiver* (1931), which wasn't exactly the kind of role a wannabe-actor yearned to portray.

All was not lost because of *The Big Trail*, however. During this time, Wayne perfected his persona as a Western actor. In over a dozen low budget films in the 1930's (and by his own account upwards of 80), John Wayne portrayed the typical machismo characteristic of the then-developing Western film.

Yakima Canutt

At a personal level too, Wayne developed the character type he would later play in films. The man of action who saves the day was the character Wayne would play repeatedly. Wayne learned the skill set necessary for the parts too, including riding a horse and drawing and toting guns.

Wayne learned at the feet of rodeo stuntman Yakima Canutt. It also helped that the characters Wayne played on screen usually had the exact same traits as the actor did off-screen. As one of his friends noted of the 6'4, muscular Wayne, "Duke's personality and sense of humor were very close to what the general public saw on the big screen. It is perhaps best shown in these words he had engraved on a plaque: 'Each of us is a mixture of some good and some not so good qualities. In considering one's fellow man it's important to remember the good things ... We should refrain from making judgments just because a fella happens to be a dirty, rotten SOB.'"

Though Wayne's professional advancement was seemingly on hold, he was at least earning money despite the Great Depression. Though he did not have A-list jobs, his B-list work was consistent, and he was able to earn a living. This allowed his personal life to advance in ways his professional life could not.

In the late 1920's, Wayne began courting a woman named Josephine Alicia Saenz. Saenz's family, however, was Roman Catholic, and thus did not approve of John Wayne's courtship of Josephine. Once Wayne was able to earn additional money, however, he was able to convince Josephine's family otherwise, and the two met significantly less resistance to their relationship. In 1933, the couple was married, and they would go on to have four children: Michael, Mary Antonia, Patrick and Melinda. Michael would become a film producer and Patrick became an actor.

However, the relationship between the newlyweds was strained from the start. To earn the income he did in B-list movies, Wayne had to work very long hours, leaving his wife to care for four small four children on her own.

Chapter 4: Stagecoach

Near the end of the decade, Wayne had spent most of the decade being typecast in a way that certainly did not suit him. As he recalled:

"They made me a singing cowboy. The fact that I couldn't sing—or play the guitar—became terribly embarrassing to me, especially on personal appearances. Every time I made a public appearance, the kids insisted that I sing The Desert Song or something. But I couldn't take along the fella who played the guitar out on one side of the camera and the fella who sang on the other side of the camera. So finally I went to the head of the studio and said. "Screw this, I can't handle it." And I quit doing those kind of pictures. They went out and brought the best hillbilly recording artist in the country to Hollywood to take my place. For the first couple of pictures, they had a hard time selling him, but he finally caught on. His name was Gene Autry. It was 1939 before I made Stagecoach—the picture that really made me a star."

As he alluded to, John Wayne's next big break came thanks to John Ford, and it came as the fitting bookend to a decade that started with his first big break. In 1939, Ford began filming the movie Wayne later identified as one of his best: the classic Western *Stagecoach*. To the great surprise of many, he chose Wayne to be the movie's star, refusing to relent when a studio head asked that he replace Wayne with Gary Cooper.

Stagecoach was a major film breakthrough for more than just John Wayne. For Ford, the film was his first outdoor Western that utilized sound recordings, after a long career spent working with silent films. Mastering dialogue, conversation and sound was thus critical to success. In the end, the combined Ford-Wayne team rose to the challenge and created a hit.

Filmed in Arizona's Monument Valley, the film could not have been set in a more ideal landscape for the Western genre. Monument Valley is replete with tall, imposing and barren rock structures, and this Martian landscape, rough and hostile to human existence, came to form the quintessential backdrop to the American Western film.

In *Stagecoach*, Wayne played Ringo Kid, a fugitive on the run whose role was second only to the film's main character, a prostitute played by Claire Trevor. Trevor was the more esteemed actress at the time, and she was given top billing by Ford in an effort to secure the necessary financing, thus relegating Wayne to sidekick status.

Today, of course, Trevor is a footnote in history. Ringo Kid may have been on the wrong side of the law, but there was a bigger enemy to deal with: Geronimo and the Apaches. Wayne's depiction of the lawless rogue was a characteristic celebration of individualism and the American spirit, and it reflected the nostalgic glorification of the old outlaws of the Wild West.

Stagecoach was a huge hit at the box office, winning two Academy Awards. Though neither went directly to John Wayne, the film's stars were catapulted to new heights, as both actor and character became essential to the emerging Western genre, complete with sound.

Chapter 5: World War II

The year 1941 shook the world of film, and the United States as a whole. That December, the surprise Japanese attack on Pearl Harbor in Hawaii immediately forced the country to join its European allies in a global and deadly war.

Hollywood was not exempt from the national preparedness that erupted after 1941, but rather than relegate Hollywood to the backburner as a distraction from more pressing concerns, national policy in the war actually promoted the film industry as one of America's strongest assets. Over the previous decade, "film" and "American" had come to be synonymous: film was quickly becoming a distinctly American form of art, the nation's contribution to human creativity.

A number of Hollywood's biggest starts left the silver screen to fight overseas. Clark Gable might not have fought off the Yankees in Gone with the Wind, but he flew for them in several B-17 bombing missions over Europe. Charlie Chaplin, who would later be accused of "Un-American activities," tried to join the Allies but did not meet the physical requirements.

Meanwhile, other actors started the tradition of giving live performances for troops on active duty overseas, a practice that stars have embraced ever since. During World War II, the "United Service Organizations" (USOs) formed across the country to support the war effort. The USOs eventually garnered support from Hollywood stars and other performers, including Bob Hope, Humphrey Bogart, Lauren Bacall and Fred Astaire. The USOs started hosting live performances at military bases overseas to boost troops' morale.

Wayne was in his mid-30s when the nation entered the war; he therefore was not drafted and did not need to serve militarily. Wayne still actually wanted to serve, but his film career limited his options, since he was contractually bound to Ford and his company. When Wayne pleaded with Ford to let him serve, Ford refused and even threatened with a lawsuit. Wayne later noted:

> "I've worked in a business where it's almost a requirement to break your word if you want to survive, but whenever I signed a contract for five years or for a certain amount of money, I've always lived up to it. I figured that if I was silly enough to sign it, or if I thought it was worth while at the time, that's the way she goes. I'm not saying that I won't drive as hard a bargain as I can. In fact, I think more about that end of the business than I did before, ever since 1959, when I found that my business manager was playing more than he was working."

Though he couldn't join the forces, that didn't mean he couldn't visit with them. Wayne, who by then was already one of America's biggest film stars, and a quintessential American hero in film, toured the Pacific and visited with troops in 1943-44. He may not have fought at Iwo Jima, but by the end of the decade he would help make the battle more famous for those who had. Nevertheless, Wayne's inability to serve gnawed at him for the rest of his life, and at least one of his wives speculated that he tried to overcompensate for it by vocalizing his patriotism over the next few decades.

Behind the scenes, John Wayne's personal life had also taken a new twist. During a film production in 1940, he had met actress Marlene Dietrich, and the two became romantically involved despite Wayne's being a married man. The relationship carried on for some time, though it ended by 1942, and the pair remained close friends.

Dietrich

Chapter 6: John Wayne the Producer

With the end of World War II in 1945, the country switched direction, and so did John Wayne professionally and personally. Just as war in Europe and Japan was coming to a close, so was Wayne's marriage. Wayne and Josephine had been separated since 1943, citing differences over how to raise their children, but Wayne's infidelity likely played a role in Josephine's change of heart. By 1945, the two filed for divorce and split separate ways, never returning.

While Wayne's marriage to Josephine had its issues, Wayne's next marriage would be even stormier. After they were divorced, he went on to marry Mexican actress Esperanza Baur, who he met in 1941 while still married to Josephine. When John and Josephine divorced in December 1945, John and Esperanza married in January 1946.

It was a bad match from the start, and Wayne later described their marriage as being "like shaking two volatile chemicals in a jar." Esperanza was jealous, a bad characteristic given the occupation and reputation of her husband in the 1940s, and Wayne later described her as "a drunken partygoer who would fall down and then accuse me of pushing her." In one notorious episode, Esperanza got into a drunken rage thinking her husband was having an affair with Gail Russell, the leading lady in *Angel and the Badman*. After that film wrapped and Wayne came home late, she fired a gun at him as he walked through the door. After seven years lobbing charges of domestic violence and adultery back and forth, the two were divorced in 1954.

Wayne and Esperanza

During this period, Wayne also had his first introduction to work as a producer. Rather than star in films, Wayne helped film them, beginning in 1947 with *Angel and the Badman,* in which he both starred and produced. It broke with the traditional Westerns of the day, as the plot revolved around an injured gunfighter who begins to rethink his way of life while he convalesces with the help of a Quaker girl, ultimately renouncing his lawless past for a quiet future of farming.

Wayne and Gail Russell in *Angel and the Badman*

John Wayne Productions, as his production company was called, achieved moderate success. While it didn't break charts, it didn't completely flop, either. Still, production wasn't his first love, and he had never completely left acting during the period, so when war movies became the rage in the wake of World War II, Wayne's career (and the studios that used him) capitalized on this genre's popularity.

In 1949, Wayne performed brilliantly in the *Sands of Iwo Jima*, playing one of his most famous roles as Sergeant John Stryker, a man greatly disliked by his fellow soldiers. His performance was widely loved, so much so that Wayne received his first Academy Award nomination for Best Actor. While he didn't win the award, the nomination was significant enough, and the award was eventually given to Broderick Crawford for his role in *All The King's Men*, the very role Wayne had turned down to star in *Sands of Iwo Jima*. Over the next decade, Wayne continued to be cast as a war hero, including as a pilot in *Flying Leathernecks* (1951), *Island in the Sky* (1953), *The High and the Mighty* (1954), *The Wings of Eagles* (1957), and *Jet Pilot*

(1957).

With *Sands of Iwo Jima* and his other work in 1949, Wayne was one of the Top 10 movie stars Over the next 25 years, Wayne would be one of the box office's Top 10 movie stars every year except 1958, an incredible stretch that indicated both his popularity and durability.

Chapter 7: Getting Political

By the early 1950's, John Wayne was a leading star in Hollywood. With a national profile, Wayne decided to delve into the difficult subjects of the day, including one of prime importance among filmmakers: communism.

Shortly after World War II, Congress' House Committee on Un-American Activities began investigating Americans across the country for suspected ties to Communism. The most famous victims of these witch hunts were Hollywood actors, such as Charlie Chaplin, whose "Un-American activity" was being neutral at the beginning of World War II. However, Elizabeth Bentley, a former communist, notified the Committee about one suspected spy ring and named several names, including Alger Hiss. Hiss was a prominent New Dealer who served on the American delegation to the San Francisco Conference that established the United Nations, and he strongly denied being a Communist, much less a spy. A former communist named Whittaker Chambers also accused Hiss of being in his Communist group, and again Hiss denied it. Eventually, Hiss was convicted of perjury when it was shown he had been a member of the Communist party in the mid-1930s, but in spite of the FBI's best efforts, its special agents never developed definitive proof that Hiss was a spy. Controversy swirled for decades over the charges, and for many the Hiss case was proof of Cold War anti-Communist hysteria.

Nevertheless, during the early part of the decade, many came under suspicion, especially in Hollywood. Given the liberal leanings of its workers, many thought Hollywood was thoroughly infiltrated with communist sympathizers. Wayne, of course, was a fervent anti-Communist who spearheaded his public opposition of it in the 1952 film *The Big Jim McLain*. In this film, he played the role of an investigator in the infamous House Committee on Un-American Activities. This committee, infamous for "Red Baiting," quickly became unpopular across the country, but was always deeply resisted in Hollywood's hills.

Off screen, Wayne worked with the few other anti-communist Hollywood actors he could find. These included the future President of the United States, Ronald Reagan. Together, the two and others formed groups like the Motion Picture Alliance for the Preservation of American Ideals. For a time, John Wayne served as the group's president.

By the end of the '50s, anti-Communism and McCarthyism had fallen into disrepute, and when Wayne later became even more outspoken as a conservative in later years, he was pressed on his anti-Communist stance and his association with the Motion Picture Alliance for the Preservation of American Ideals in the Playboy interview:

Playboy: Was the Motion Picture Alliance formed to blacklist Communists and Communist sympathizers?

Wayne: Our organization was just a group of motion-picture people on the right side, not leftists and not Commies. I was the president for a couple of years. There was no blacklist at that time, as some people said. That was a lot of horseshit. Later on, when Congress passed some laws making it possible to take a stand against these people, we were asked about Communists in the industry. So we gave them the facts as we knew them. That's all. The only thing our side did that was anywhere near blacklisting was just running a lot of people out of the business.

Playboy: That sounds a good deal worse than blacklisting. Why couldn't you permit all points of view to be expressed freely on the screen?

Wayne: Because it's been proven that communism is foreign to the American way of life. If you'd read the official Communist doctrine and then listened to the arguments of these people we were opposing, you'd find they were reciting propaganda by rote. Besides, these Communist sympathizers ran a lot of our people out of the business. One of them was a Pulitzer Prize winner who's now a columnist—Morrie Ryskind. They just never used him again at MGM after Dore Schary took charge of the studio, even though he was under contract.

Playboy: What was the mood in Hollywood that made it so fashionable to take such a vigorous stand against communism?

Wayne: Many of us were being invited to supposed social functions or house parties—usually at well-known Hollywood writers' homes—that turned out to be Communist recruitment meetings. Suddenly, everybody from makeup men to stagehands found themselves in seminars on Marxism. Take this colonel I knew, the last man to leave the Philippines on a submarine in 1942. He came back here and went to work sending food and gifts to U.S. prisoners on Bataan. He'd already gotten a Dutch ship that was going to take all this stuff over. The State Department pulled him off of it and sent the poor bastard out to be the technical director on my picture Back to Bataan, which was being made by Eddie Dmytryk. I knew that he and a whole group of actors in the picture were pro-Reds, and when I wasn't there, these pro-Reds went to work on the colonel. He was a Catholic, so they kidded him about his religion: They even sang the Internationale at lunchtime. He finally came to me and said, "Mr. Wayne, I haven't anybody to turn to. These people are doing everything in their power to belittle me." So I went to Dmytryk and said, "Hey, are you a Commie?" He said, "No, I'm not a Commie. My father was a Russian. I was born in Canada. But if the masses of the American people want communism, I think it'd be good for our country." When he used the word "masses," he exposed himself. That word is not a part of Western terminology. So I knew he was a Commie. Well, it later came out that he was.

I also knew two other fellas who really did things that were detrimental to our way of life. One of them was Carl Foreman, the guy who wrote the screenplay for High Noon, and the other was Robert Rossen, the one who made the picture about Huey Long, All the King's Men. In Rossen's version of All the King's Men, which he sent me to read for a part, every character who had any responsibility at all was guilty of some offense against society. To make Huey Long a wonderful, rough pirate was great; but, according to this picture, everybody was a shit except for this weakling intern doctor who was trying to find a place in the world. I sent the script back to Charlie Feldman, my agent, and said, "If you ever send me a script like this again, I'll fire you." Ironically, it won the Academy Award.

High Noon was even worse. Everybody says High Noon is a great picture because Tiomkin wrote some great music for it and because Gary Cooper and Grace Kelly were in it. So it's got everything going for it. In that picture, four guys come in to gun down the sheriff. He goes to the church and asks for help and the guys go, "Oh well, oh gee." And the women stand up and say, "You're rats. You're rats. You're rats." So Cooper goes out alone. It's the most un-American thing I've ever seen in my whole life. The last thing in the picture is ole Coop putting the United States marshal's badge under his foot and stepping on it. I'll never regret having helped run Foreman out of this country.

Chapter 8: The Quiet Man

Though Wayne was fervently pro-American, he took some time in the early 1950's to pay homage to his Irish roots. He did so alongside fellow Irish-American actress, Maureen O'Hara. Wayne would spend much of the '40s and '50s working with O'Hara, another rising star of the American (and Irish) film industry, most notably in *She Wore A Yellow Ribbon* (1949) and *Rio Grande* (1950).

O'Hara

The 1950's were not just an era of Cold War "Red Baiting". Americans of all colors also came to respect their ethnic roots. For millions of Americans, this pointed them towards Ireland. Across the Atlantic, Ireland was increasingly engaged in a conflict with its English neighbors, but amid that strife, the Irish reciprocated their diaspora's appreciation from across the Atlantic by recognizing the important and deep Irish-American historical connections.

This mutual admiration helped spawn one of Wayne's most unusual movies, *The Quiet Man*. In it, Wayne played the role of Sean Thorton, a second generation Irish-American who has returned to Inisfree, Ireland, to reclaim his family's estate. His trip, however, offers him more than just property. There he meets Mary Kate Danaher, played by Maureen O'Hara, an Irish woman living with her brother. The pair falls in love, but Mary Kate's family refuses to consent to marriage between her and the Irish-American Thorton.

The character John Wayne played portrayed everything that was characteristic of Irish-America. He was a boxer and a devout Roman Catholic from Pennsylvania who lived in an old industrial town. His parents left Ireland during the Potato Famine, and the famine was always on his mind.

Though the movie was significantly American - it was directed by John Ford - it was more successful abroad in Ireland and Great Britain. It received Academy Award nominations and even won two - best director and best cinematography. John Wayne, however, did not bring home an award and still had yet to receive any during his career. His day at the top was yet to come.

Chapter 9: The Searchers

The 1950's were an era of American nostalgia. Victory in World War II had positioned America as the world's most powerful country. In response to this national euphoria, traditional "Americana" themes surged in popularity. Westerns, John Wayne's beloved genre, were a critical part of this resurgence.

This culminated in 1956, with the release of the John Ford-directed film *The Searchers*. Set during the Texas-Indian Wars, the movie featured classic scenes of American frontier life, particularly the rough and tumble lawless society. Wayne fused war hero and Westerner together as Ethan Edwards, a Confederate veteran in search of a lost niece. Though set in Texas, Ford used his now-classic setting, Arizona's Monument Valley.

Upon its release, *The Searchers* was an instant success, earning nearly $5 million dollars and quickly receiving much critical acclaim. By the time Academy Awards were announced, however, *The Searchers* fell short. Critics thought it too violent and kitschy to be deserving of an Academy Award, even though the American people and viewers abroad loved the movie. Wayne would later call *The Searchers* one of his greatest movies and noted he didn't think the movie got the critical acclaim it deserved. Wayne even named one of his sons Ethan after the character he played in the movie.

Wayne in *The Searchers*

Though movie critics at the time thought the movie was relatively insignificant, *The Searchers* has since come to occupy a prominent place in the American film canon. It is now widely considered not only one of the best Western films, but one of the most defining and important American films ever shot. And with it, Wayne's performance has been universally praised as one of his finest.

Wayne's career had reached new heights, but his personal life reached new lows. For a second time, his marriage was crumbling, and in 1954, Wayne and his wife Esperanza divorced. Within less than a year of the divorce, Wayne remarried, this time to Pilar Pallete, a Peruvian actress 29 years his junior. The couple would have three children: Aissa Wayne, John Ethan Wayne, and Marisa Wayne.

Wayne and Pallete

Chapter 10: The 1960s

John Wayne opened a new decade with one of his most iconic films, *The Alamo*, which he also directed. Based on one of the most famous battles in American history, *The Alamo* portrayed Sam Houston and his battle for Texas against the Mexicans. Of course, Wayne did not simply direct the film; he played a leading role as Davy Crockett, a classic frontier folk hero. Wayne had hoped to play Sam Houston, who had a smaller role and thus would have allowed Wayne more time to perfect his directing, but naturally the studio heads wanted him to have a prominent role in the film as well.

Despite having to act in a starring role, Wayne directed a film that would later be nominated for Best Picture. His daughter Aissa later attributed Wayne's fine and intense directing work to the fact that he treated it like he was actually fighting for the cause, noting, "I think making The Alamo became my father's own form of combat. More than an obsession, it was the most intensely personal project in his career." Naturally, his hands-on directing got on some of the actors' nerves at times, and it was noted that Wayne rewrote some of the actors' lines, particularly to hammer his pro-American themes. At one point, Wayne's Crockett exhorts, "Republic. I like the sound of the word. Means that people can live free, talk free, go or come, buy or sell, be drunk or sober, however they choose. Some words give you a feeling. Republic is one of those words that makes me tight in the throat." When Wayne himself was asked about what statement he was trying to make in *The Alamo*, he responded, "I thought it would be a tremendous epic picture that would say 'America.'"

   Though the film was a huge box office success, it was not necessarily the success Wayne and other hoped it would be. The producers had literally created a village and an almost full-scale model replica of the Alamo itself. The huge cost of production - over $12 million dollars - meant that the bar was raised high in terms of expectations, and Wayne was so involved with the project that he helped finance it with $1.5 million of his own money. Many expected it to exceed sales of $12 million, a large sum at the time, but the film fell short, and Wayne lost much of his personal investment in the film.

The set's version of the Alamo. Photograph by Larry D. Moore

   Among movie critics, the reception was mixed, however. Some thought it fell flat, portraying a well-known and unoriginal narrative, and Wayne's insistence on having characters give pro-American soliloquies made some wince. Others marveled at the cinematography, particularly the climactic final battle. In the end, the movie was good enough to at least win a few Academy Awards, and be nominated for many more. Wayne himself received his second nomination for

Best Director, but again he fell short, losing to Billy Wilder and *The Apartment.* Elsewhere, though, the movie won the Academy Award for Best Sound and was nominated for Best Cinematography, Best Film Editing, Best Music (Song), Best Music (Lyrics) and Best Picture.

How The West Was Won

With a series of films in which his acting and directing won accolades, and his star power, Wayne was ready to take on new roles during the '60s. Though *The Alamo* had received mixed reviews, Wayne's next big hit was decidedly more popular. John Ford's *The Man Who Shot Liberty Valance* (1962) cast Wayne as the main character, a local rancher named Tom Doniphon. Though filmed in the early 60's, *The Man Who Shot Liberty Valance* was filmed in black and white. With scenes of bars, drunkeness, lawlessness and corrupt politicians, the movie was like a throwback to the Westerns Wayne had become so familiar with over two decades earlier.

That same year, John Wayne also starred in *The Longest Day,* which was also produced in black and white and featured an enormously large cast, one of the biggest of its time. Unlike the Westerns Wayne had become accustomed to, this film was a war drama, another genre that became closely associated with him. Based on the D-Day invasion, the film portrayed the landings on Normandy June 6, 1944.

Perhaps his greatest contribution of the early 60's, *How the West Was Won* wrapped together the Western and war genres that had made Wayne the most popular actor of his generation. Spanning generations, the epic movie had an ensemble cast that told the story of Americans opening up the frontier, and in the film Wayne played General William Tecumseh Sherman, the famous Union general instrumental in winning the Civil War. Throughout the movie, Sherman and Grant have to worry about attempts on their lives by Southern partisan outlaws hoping their deaths would turn the tide of the war in the Confederacy's favor.

Cancer

Wayne was still at the height of his professional success, but he had rarely made good choices in his personal life. This had been evident in his personal relationships with his various wives, but by the mid-60s, it was apparent that his choices had also detrimentally affected his health.

Since his late teens, John Wayne was a hard drinker, perhaps not surprising given the characters he played. It was said that directors tried to shoot Wayne's scenes before noon, so that they would not run the risk that he was drunk on the set. Moreover, he had been a ravenous chain smoker, which didn't necessarily set him apart in his era, but throughout the 50s and 60s the public health problems associated with smoking were just beginning to be widely known. In the 1950s, Wayne had performed for the Camel Company in advertisements for cigarettes, and by some accounts he even smoked as much as six packs a day.

In 1964, doctors found a baseball-sized tumor on his left lung, and diagnosed the famous actor with lung cancer. Doctors had found a large tumor that would require an extremely risky surgery, and the actor didn't have a very positive prognosis. Rather than endure a tumor removal and chemotherapy, doctors thought the best option for Wayne was to simply remove his left lung. The operation would leave him unable to perform the rigorous and physically demanding roles of his younger years, but it left hope that at least he might survive. Wayne recalled:

"Well, I had two operations six days apart—one for a cancer that was as big as a baby's fist, and then one for edema. I wasn't so uptight when I was told about the cancer. My biggest fear came when they twisted my windpipe and had to sew me back together a second time. When my family came in to see me and I saw the looks on their faces, I figured, "Well, Jeez, I must be just about all through."

Though lung cancer survival was rare – and remains uncommon today – Wayne's lung removal was successful. His recovery, however, was hardly quick. It took five years for Wayne to become cancer-free, and in 1969, with one lung less, John Wayne was cancer- and cigarette-free. He did, however, replace cigarettes with chewing tobacco, which at the time seemed liked a health alternative. When asked how he kept up his spirits, Wayne explained:

"By thinking about God and my family and my friends and telling myself, "Everything will be all right." And it was. I licked the big C. I know the man upstairs will pull the plug when he wants to, but I don't want to end up my life being sick. I want to go out on two feet—in action."

Producers and advertisers around John Wayne did not want him to go public with his illness. Because he had advertised for smoking companies, many thought his public announcement would sink sales and destroy the cigarette industry. Regardless of this feedback, Wayne did go public with his illness. Not only did he go public, but he also did anti-smoking commercials for cancer and anti-smoking organizations. In doing so, he became a very public advocate for cancer awareness.

1968

The year 1968 was a traumatic one for the United States, but for the world. The dual assassinations of Martin Luther King and Robert Kennedy shook the United States, while anti-war protests across Western Europe and the U.S. threatened to overturn law and order.

With interest in the Vietnam War waning, John Wayne hoped to use his public status to rally support for the cause. To do so, he produced, directed, and starred in *The Green Berets*, an anti-Communist themed movie that tried to portray the glory of the Vietnam War. Unfortunately, the movie fell flat; anti-war sentiment had turned too quickly against Vietnam for a movie to change public opinion, no matter who starred in it.

When asked why *The Green Berets* was panned by critics and flopped with audiences, Wayne took a swipe at the critics for playing politics:

> "Because the critics don't like my politics, and they were condemning the war, not the picture. I don't mean the critics as a group. I mean the irrationally liberal ones. Renata Adler of The New York Times almost foamed at the mouth because I showed a few massacres on the screen. She went into convulsions. She and other critics wouldn't believe that the Viet Cong are treacherous—that the dirty sons of bitches are raping, torturing gorillas. In the picture, I repeated the story General Stilwell told me about this South Vietnamese mayor. The V.C. tied him up and brought his wife out and about 40 men raped her; and then they brought out his two teenage daughters, hung them upside down and gutted them in front of him. And then they took an iron rod and beat on his wife until every bone in her goddamn body was broken. That's torture, I'd say. So I mentioned this in the picture, and the critics were up in arms about that… Luckily for me, they overkilled it. The Green Berets would have been successful regardless of what the critics did, but it might have taken the public longer to find out about the picture if they hadn't made so much noise about it."

With his illness having hampered him and *The Green Berets* flopping, Wayne had to worry that his incredibly long and successful career might be drawing to a close. At the same time, however, many in the Republican Party thought the ultra-conservative Wayne was a suitable figure to run for public office. Supporters in Texas and fellow actors in public offices egged Wayne on to run for Vice President of the United States, and the notorious segregationist George Wallace asked him to be his vice-presidential candidate for his independent run in 1968. Of course, the run would be more symbolic than substantive, but some thought it had serious potential. Wayne was also busy filming *True Grit* at the time, and besides, he considered himself a Nixon supporter.

Wayne, though an avid political junkie, thought the idea a bad one. He could not imagine an actor in the White House, though he ironically devoted much of 1968 to supporting fellow actor-turned-politician Ronald Reagan in governing the state of California as Governor. He also actively campaigned for Richard Nixon's successful race for the White House. Wayne left his mark without having to occupy a public office.

True Grit

Despite his lung removal, John Wayne's career actually reached its apex in the late '60s with the hit film *True Grit*. It would win him his only Academy Award.

After the murder of Frank Ross by his hired hand, Ross's teenage daughter hopes to track down his assassin. To do so, she seeks out the assistance of John Wayne's character, "Rooster" Cogburn. Cogburn was a well-known investigator capable of tracking down the murderer and bringing justice to the young girl.

The quest takes them through a wild and lawless Western Territory, including Indian Territory, in modern-day Oklahoma. The path takes them through cacti, rattlesnakes and lawless murderers. After injury and defeat, the pair finds the murderer, Chaney, with the young girl, Mattie, proving to be an able assistant.

John Wayne performed well in the production of *True Grit*. Of the script, he said it was one of the best he'd ever read. In addition, he fell in love with one of the horses that he rode during the film's production.

Many had low expectations for Wayne due to his lung loss, but ever the man's man, Wayne barely missed a step. After the lung removal, Wayne noted, "The operation hasn't impeded anything except that I get short of breath quickly. Particularly in the higher altitudes, that slows me down. I still do my own fights and all that stuff. I'd probably do a little bit more if I had more wind, but I still do more than my share. Nobody else does anything any more than I do, whether they're young or old."

Indeed, he proved critics wrong in a big way with *True Grit*. Despite numerous Academy Award nominations, John Wayne had never actually won an award until *True Grit* in 1969. That year, he finally won the Best Actor award. He also won a Golden Globe Award for his performance.

Years later, in 2010, Wayne's performance was admirably honored with a remake of the original film. That year, a second *True Grit* movie was produced, paying homage to John Wayne's place in the history of American Western Film.

Chapter 11: Final Years

The early 1970's brought John Wayne's involvement with politics to a new height. It also proved to be one of his last interventions in public affairs.

In 1971, John Wayne gave his now famous (or infamous) interview to *Playboy Magazine*, and his candid, outspoken answers on the hot political topics of the day transformed his image almost overnight. The *Playboy* interview touched on critical topics of race and sex in American society. Of African-Americans, John Wayne said hostile things like "I believe in white supremacy until the blacks are educated to a point of responsibility." When asked how blacks might get the background they need to become "responsible," Wayne replied "By going to school. I don't know why people insist that blacks have been forbidden their right to go to school. They were allowed in public schools wherever I've been." To another question about anti-African American discrimination in Hollywood, Wayne said "Oh, Christ no. I've directed two pictures and I gave the blacks their proper position. I had a black slave in The Alamo." With the Civil Rights Movement churning nationwide, these words weren't exactly well-received by the American public.

Wayne was also outspoken on Vietnam in a way that made him seem both out of touch and past his time:

Playboy: Many of those young men who "own a piece of that war" never wanted to go to Vietnam in the first place. Do you think our government is justified in sending them off to fight in an undeclared war?

Wayne: Well, I sure don't know why we send them over to fight and then stop the bombing so they can get shot that much more. We could easily stop the enemy from getting guns and ammunition that we know are being sent by Chinese and Soviet Communists. But we won't do anything to stop it because we're afraid of world opinion. Why in hell should we worry about world opinion when we're trying to help out a country that's asked for our aid? Of course, Senator Fulbright says the South Vietnamese government doesn't represent the people—even though it's been duly elected by those people. How can a man be so swayed to the opposite side? If he were finding fault with the administration of our help over there, that I could understand. What I can't understand is this "pull out, pull out, pull out" attitude he's taken. And what makes it worse is that a lot of people accept anything he says without thinking, simply because the Fulbright scholarships have established an intellectual aura around him.

Playboy: Three Presidents seem to have agreed that it would be unwise to gamble millions of lives on that assumption. Since you find their leadership lacking, who would you have preferred in the highest office?

Wayne: Barry Goldwater would at least have been decisive. I know for a fact that he's a truthful man. Before the '64 election, he told me that he said to the Texan, "I don't think we ought to make an issue out of Vietnam because we both know that we're going to probably end up having to send a half a million men over there." Johnson said, "Yeah, that's probably true, Barry, but I've got an election to win." So Barry told the truth and Johnson got elected on a "peace" platform—and then began to ease them in, a few thousand at a time. I wish our friend Fulbright would bring out those points. If

Douglas MacArthur were alive, he also would have handled the Vietnam situation with dispatch. He was a proven administrator, certainly a proven leader. And MacArthur understood what Americans were and what Americans stood for. Had he been elected President, something significant would have happened during his administration. He would have taken a stand for the United States in world affairs, and he would have stood by it, and we would have been respected for it. I also admired the tie salesman. President Truman. He was a wonderful, feisty guy who'll go down in history as quite an individual. It's a cinch he had great guts when he decided to straighten things out in Korea; it's just too bad that the State Department was able to frighten him out of doing a complete job. Seems to me, politics have entered too much into the decisions of our leadership. I can't understand politicians. They're either yellowing out from taking a stand or using outside pressure to improve their position.

Nearing the end of his career, Wayne's later political comments left a sour taste in many Americans' minds. His statements on race made him appear to be out of step with society and the times, not to mention an outright racist. Wayne became the archconservative elephant in the room, not the actor who defined the image and swagger of the American hero. Prominent "Yippie" Abbie Hoffman summed up many Americans' view of Wayne in his final years, "I like Wayne's wholeness, his style. As for his politics, well — I suppose even cavemen felt a little admiration for the dinosaurs that were trying to gobble them up." And controversy aside, one movie critic reviewing 1972's *The Cowboys* wrote of the actor, "Wayne is, of course, marvelously indestructible, and he has become an almost perfect father figure."

He may have been a perfect father figure on the big screen, but Wayne's third marriage was falling apart. In 1973, he and his third wife separated, though they never divorced. Disagreements over numerous things had taken their toll on the marriage, and Wayne would take up an affair with another woman for the rest of his life.

Wayne and Pilar Pallete in 1971

Final Film

   John Wayne's final film came in the year 1976, the same year his political arch-enemy –
Jimmy Carter – was elected President. Fittingly, it was a classic Western called *The Shootist*,
which began with a piece that paid homage to the actor himself by showing a montage of
previous scenes of his from other movies. And true to himself and his roles, Wayne insisted that
one scene in the movie be changed because he refused to have his character shoot somebody in
the back. "I've made over 250 pictures and have never shot a guy in the back. Change it."

By 1976, Wayne's health was very poor, and many doubted his ability to complete his role in *The Shootist.* Nevertheless, Wayne starred as J.B. Books, an old and dying man who is also witnessing the death of the "Old West." The movie looks back fondly on the days of the Wild West, and examines the region's transition into a more mainstream part of American society.

The story of *The Shootist* and the role Wayne played could not have been a more fitting culmination of a film career spanning decades. Wayne's character was dying of cancer and mourning the loss of an era. Meanwhile, Wayne himself was dying – though he had no diagnosed cancer at the time – and interest in the Western genre was also dying. Thus, Wayne's character was a reflection of himself, in a way none of his previous films was able to accomplish.

The Shootist, despite waning interest in Westerns, was well-received by movie critics and was nominated for both an Academy Award and a Golden Globe though it did not win any awards. Regardless, it was a great way for John Wayne to finish his movie career.

Death

Though Wayne was technically not diagnosed with cancer during the filming of *The Shootist*, he was physically weak and generally unhealthy. A few years later, in 1979, Wayne arrived at the Emergency Room for what he thought were issues with his gallbladder. After some investigation, doctors discovered that the actor's gallbladder was not the problem: he had a huge cancerous tumor on his stomach. Doctors immediately removed the tumor in a nine and a half hour operation, and Wayne survived for some months.

That April, Wayne was well enough to attend the Golden Globe Awards. The media and everyone in attendance, however, know that Wayne was not well. Less than a month later, Wayne arrived back in the hospital, this time to discover that cancer had spread to his intestines. The prognosis was not good.

Wayne was in total agony during the final months of his life. The prognosis, however, was apparent: Wayne's life would only last a few short weeks.

President Jimmy Carter, despite his political differences with John Wayne, visited the actor at his bedside, and Queen Elizabeth II sent him a get well card. All the well wishes in the world, however, could not save John Wayne, and the legendary actor passed away on June 11, 1979, at the age of 72.

Though a legendary actor, Wayne's recurring battle with cancer has also played a critical role in the actor's legacy. The John Wayne Cancer Institute was founded in his honor to research and provide care to those suffering from cancer.

Though Wayne and the Westerns of his day have faded from public eye, it is indisputable that he continues to be a household name and an iconic symbol of a certain type of America everyone is familiar with, for better or for worse. John Wayne is America's actor, defining a genre and a movement, and his legacy lives on in the reels of Hollywood's archives and the living rooms of Middle America.

John Wayne Filmography

1926-1940

Brown of Harvard	Yale Football Player
Bardelys the Magnificent	Guard
The Great K & A Train Robbery	extra
Annie Laurie	extra
The Drop Kick (US title) Glitter (GB title)	extra
Mother Machree	extra
Four Sons	extra
Hangman's House	Horse Race Spectator/Condemned Man

Noah's Ark	Flood Extra
Speakeasy	extra
The Black Watch	extra
Words and Music	Pete Donahue
Salute	Bill, Midshipman
The Forward Pass	extra
Men Without Women	Radioman on surface
Born Reckless	Soldier
Rough Romance	Lumberjack
Cheer Up and Smile	bit part
The Big Trail	Breck Coleman
Girls Demand Excitement	Peter Brooks
Three Girls Lost	Gordon Wales
Arizona (US title)	Lt. Bob Denton

The Virtuous Wife (GB title)	
The Deceiver	Reginald Thorpe's corpse
Range Feud	Clint Turner
Maker of Men	Dusty Rhodes
The Voice of Hollywood No. 13	Himself
Running Hollywood	Himself
The Shadow of the Eagle	Craig McCoy
Texas Cyclone	Steve Pickett
Two-Fisted Law	Duke
Lady and Gent	Buzz Kinney
The Hurricane Express	Larry Baker
The Hollywood Handicap	Himself
Ride Him, Cowboy (US title)	John Drury
The Hawk (GB title)	

That's My Boy	Football Player
The Big Stampede	John Steele
Haunted Gold	John Mason
The Telegraph Trail	John Trent
The Three Musketeers	Tom Wayne
Central Airport	Co-pilot in wreck
Somewhere in Sonora	John Bishop
His Private Secretary	Dick Wallace
The Life of Jimmy Dolan(US title)	Smith
The Kid's Last Fight (GBtitle)	
Baby Face	Jimmy McCoy
The Man from Monterey	Capt. John Holmes
Riders of Destiny	Sandy Saunders ("Singing Sandy")
The Sweetheart of Sigma Chi	Bit part

College Coach (US title)	Student greeting Phil
Football Coach (GB title)	
Sagebrush Trail	John Brant
The Lucky Texan	Jerry Mason
West of the Divide	Ted Hayden
Blue Steel	John Carruthers
The Man from Utah	John Westen
Randy Rides Alone	Randy Bowers
The Star Packer	John Travers
The Trail Beyond	Rod Drew
The Lawless Frontier	John Tobin
'Neath the Arizona Skies	Chris Morrell
Texas Terror	John Higgins
Rainbow Valley	John Martin

The Desert Trail	John Scott
The Dawn Rider	John Mason
Paradise Canyon	John Wyatt
Westward Ho	John Wyatt
The New Frontier	John Dawson
Lawless Range	John Middleton
The Oregon Trail	Capt. John Delmont
The Lawless Nineties	John Tipton
King of the Pecos	John Clayborn
The Lonely Trail	Captain John Ashley
Winds of the Wasteland(AKA Stagecoach Run)	John Blair
Sea Spoilers	Bob Randall
Conflict	Pat Glendon
California Straight Ahead!	Biff Smith

I Cover the War	Bob Adams
Idol of the Crowds	Johnny Hanson
Adventure's End	Duke Slade
Born to the West (original title)	Dare Rudd
Hell Town (reissue title)	
Pals of the Saddle	Stoney Brooke
Overland Stage Raiders	Stoney Brooke
Santa Fe Stampede	Stoney Brooke
Red River Range	Stoney Brooke
Stagecoach	Henry ("The Ringo Kid")
The Night Riders	Stoney Brooke
Three Texas Steers (UStitle)	Stoney Brooke
Danger Rides the Range(GB title)	
Wyoming Outlaw	Stoney Brooke

New Frontier (original title	Stoney Brooke
Frontier Horizon (TV title)	
Allegheny Uprising (US title)	Jim Smith
The First Rebel (GB title)	
Dark Command	Bob Seton
Screen Snapshots Series 19, No. 8: Cowboy Jubilee	Himself
Three Faces West	John Phillips
The Long Voyage Home	Ole Olson
Seven Sinners (original title)	Lt. Dan Brent
Cafe of the Seven Sinners(GB re-issue title)	

1941-1960

A Man Betrayed(United States title)	Lynn Hollister
Citadel of Crime (GBtitle)	

Wheel of Fortune (TVtitle)	
Lady from Louisiana	John Reynolds
The Shepherd of the Hills	Matt Matthews
Meet the Stars: Past and Present	Himself
Lady for a Night	Jack Morgan
Reap the Wild Wind	Capt. Jack Stuart
The Spoilers	Roy Glennister
In Old California	Tom Craig
Flying Tigers	Jim Gordon
Reunion in France(United States title)	Pat Talbot
Mademoiselle France(GB title)	
Pittsburgh	Charles "Pittsburgh" Markham
A Lady Takes a Chance	Duke Hudkins

In Old Oklahoma	Dan Somers
War of the Wildcats(re-issue title)	
The Fighting Seabees	Wedge Donovan
Tall in the Saddle	Rocklin
Flame of Barbary Coast	Duke Fergus
Back to Bataan	Col. Joseph Madden
They Were Expendable	Lt. Rusty Ryan
Dakota	John Devlin
Without Reservations	Rusty Thomas
Angel and the Badman	Quirt Evans
Tycoon	Johnny Munroe
Red River	Thomas Dunson
Fort Apache	Capt. Kirby York
3 Godfathers	Robert Marmaduke

	Hightower
Wake of the Red Witch	Edward Ludwig
The Fighting Kentuckian	John Breen
She Wore a Yellow Ribbon	Capt. Nathan Brittles
Screen Snapshots: Hollywood Rodeo	Himself
Sands of Iwo Jima	Sgt. John M. Stryker
Rio Grande	Lt. Col. Kirby Yorke
Screen Snapshots: Reno's Silver Spur Awards	Himself
Operation Pacific	"Duke" Gifford
The Screen Director	Himself
Screen Snapshots: Hollywood Awards	Himself
Flying Leathernecks	Major Dan Kirby
Miracle in Motion	Narrator
The Quiet Man	Sean Thornton

Big Jim McLain	Big Jim McLain
Trouble Along the Way	Steve Aloysius Williams
Island in the Sky	Capt. Dooley
Hondo	Hondo Lane
The High and the Mighty	Dan Roman
The Sea Chase	Capt. Karl Ehrlich
Screen Snapshots: The Great Al Jolson	Himself
Blood Alley	Captain Tom Wilder
The Conqueror	Temüjin (Genghis Khan)
The Searchers	Ethan Edwards
The Wings of Eagles	Frank "Spig" Wead
Jet Pilot	Colonel Jim Shannon
Legend of the Lost	Joe January

I Married a Woman	Himself
The Barbarian and the Geisha	Townsend Harris
Rio Bravo	John T. Chance
The Horse Soldiers	Col. John Marlowe
The Alamo	Col. David Crockett
North to Alaska	Sam McCord

Wayne produced but did not star in the feature films listed below:

Title	Year
The Bullfighter and the Lady	1951
Plunder of the Sun	1953
Ring of Fear	1954
Track of the Cat	1956
Goodbye, My Lady	1956

Seven Men From Now	1956
Gun the Man Down	1956
Man in the Vault	1956
China Doll	1958
Escort West	1959
Hondo and the Apaches	1967

1961-1976

Title	Role
The Challenge of Ideas	Himself
The Comancheros	Jake Cutter
The Man Who Shot Liberty Valance	Tom Doniphon
Hatari!	Sean Mercer
The Longest Day	Lt Col. Benjamin Vandervoort

How the West Was Won	Gen. William Tecumseh Sherman[4]
Donovan's Reef	Michael Patrick Donovan
McLintock!	George Washington McLintock
Circus World(US title)	Matt Masters
The Magnificent Showman (GBtitle)	
The Greatest Story Ever Told	The Centurion (Longinus)
In Harm's Way	Capt. Rockwell Torrey
The Sons of Katie Elder	John Elder
Cast a Giant Shadow	Gen. Mike Randolph
El Dorado	Cole Thornton

A Nation Builds Under Fire	Himself
The War Wagon	Taw Jackson
The Green Berets	Col. Mike Kirby
Hellfighters	Chance Buckman
True Grit	U.S. Marshal Reuben J. "Rooster" Cogburn
The Undefeated	Col. John Henry Thomas
No Substitute for Victory	Narrator
Chisum	John Chisum
Rio Lobo	Cord McNally
Big Jake	Jacob McCandles
Directed by John Ford	Himself
The Cowboys	Wil Andersen

Cancel My Reservation	Himself
The Train Robbers	Lane
Cahill, United States Marshal (UStitle)	J.D. Cahill
Cahill (GBtitle)	
McQ	Det. Lt. Lon McQ
Brannigan	Brannigan
Rooster Cogburn	Marshal Reuben J. 'Rooster' Cogburn[10]
Chesty: Tribute to a Legend	Himself
The Shootist	John Bernard Books

Printed in Great Britain
by Amazon.co.uk, Ltd.,
Marston Gate.